Time to Get Started!

Getting It Done!

Reggie Harper

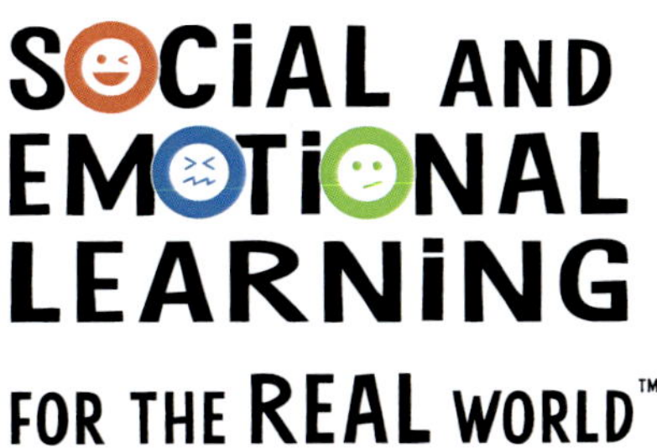

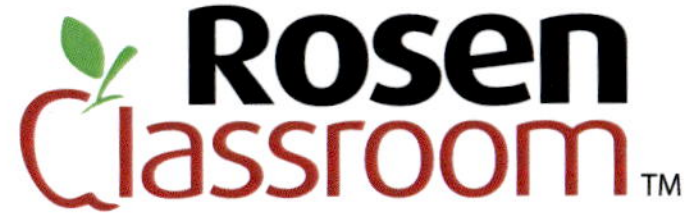

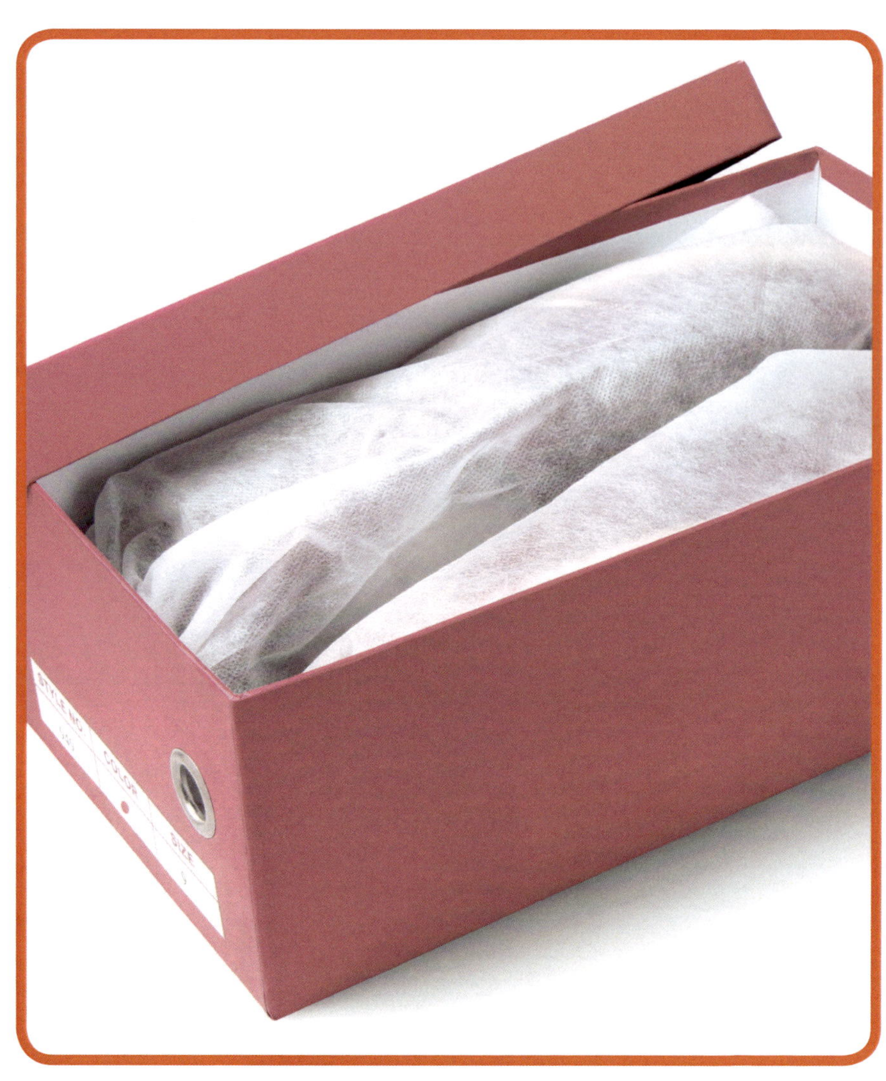

Time to start.

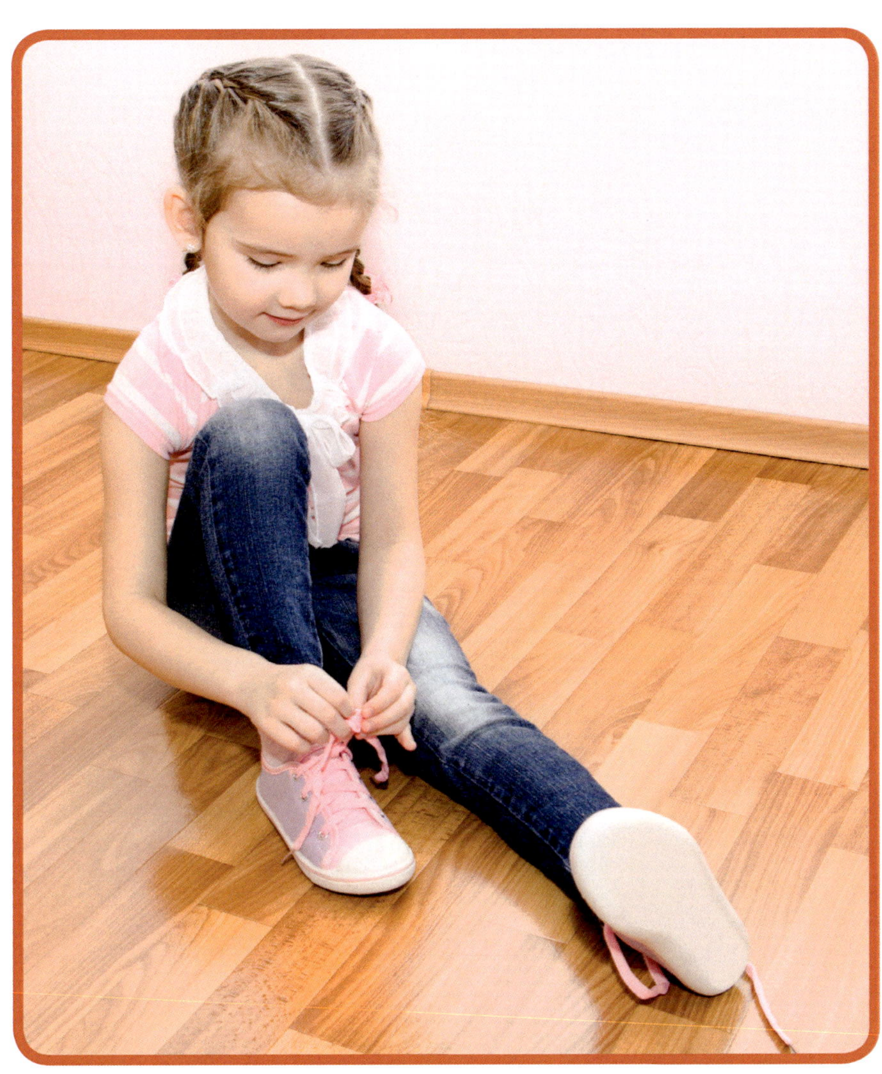

I try.

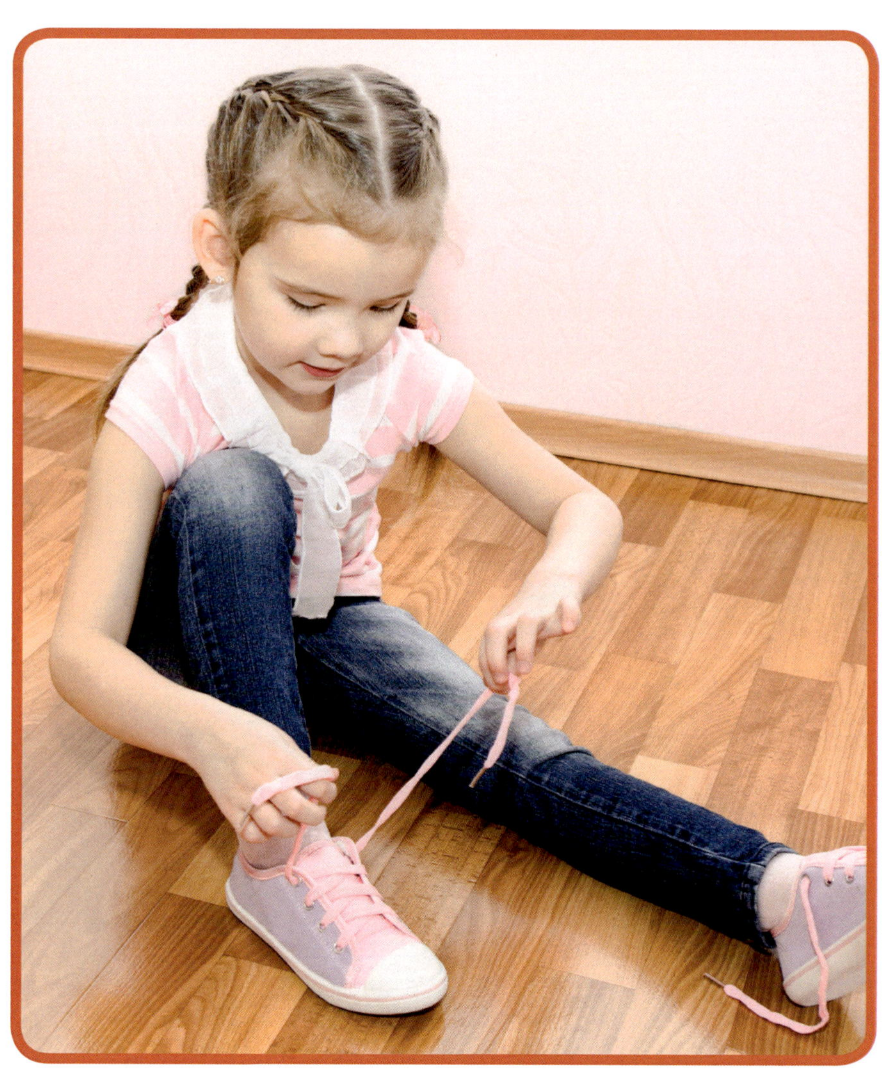

I pull.

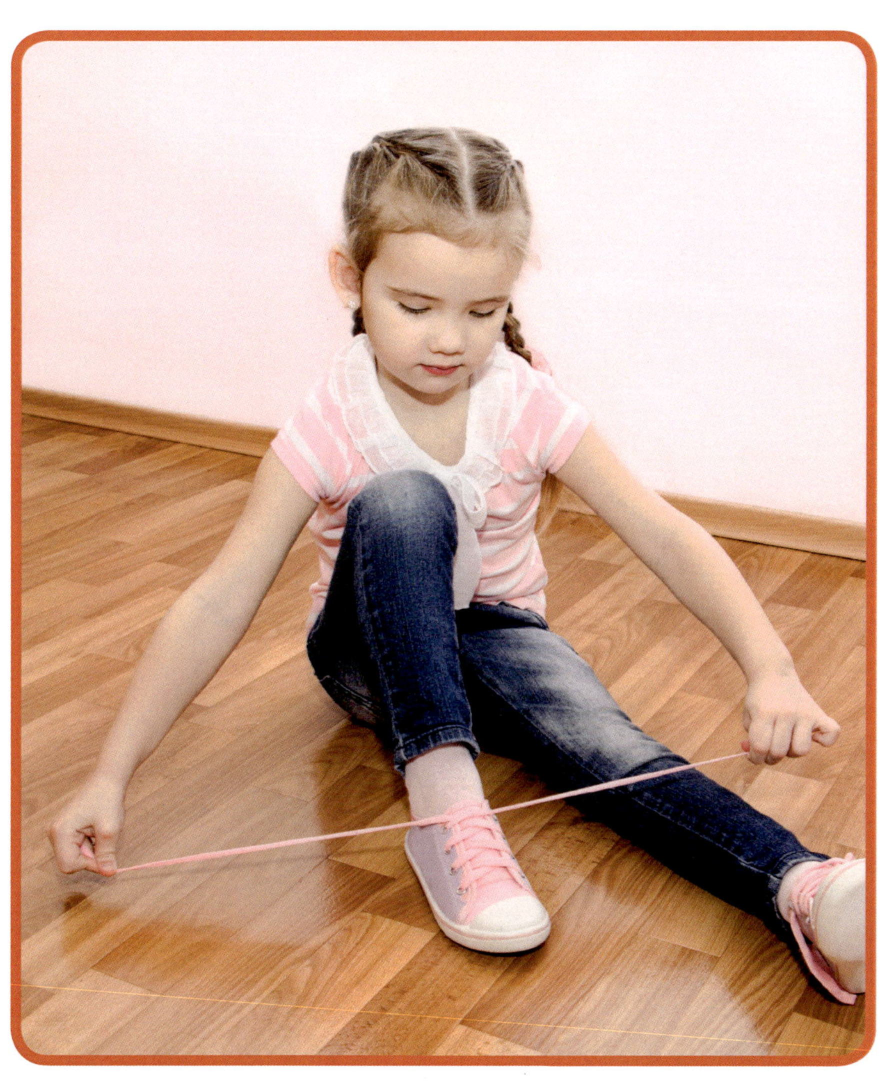

I cross.

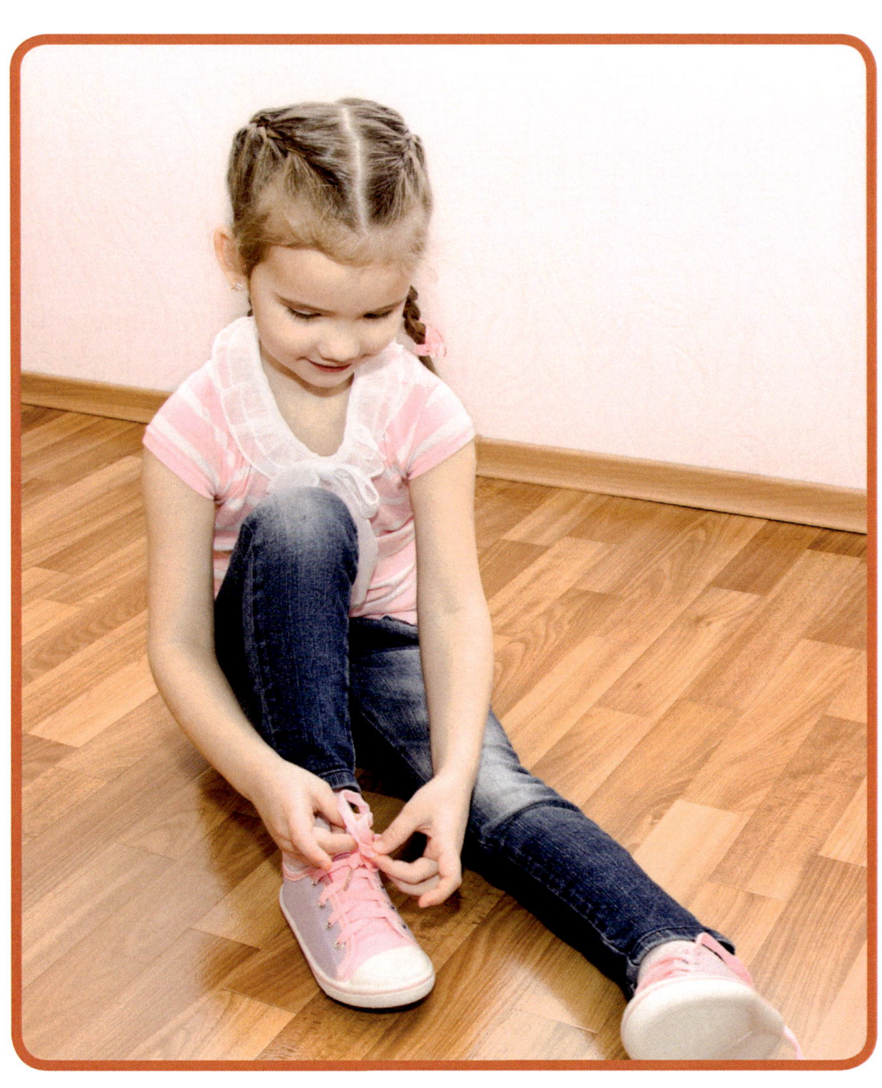

I tuck.

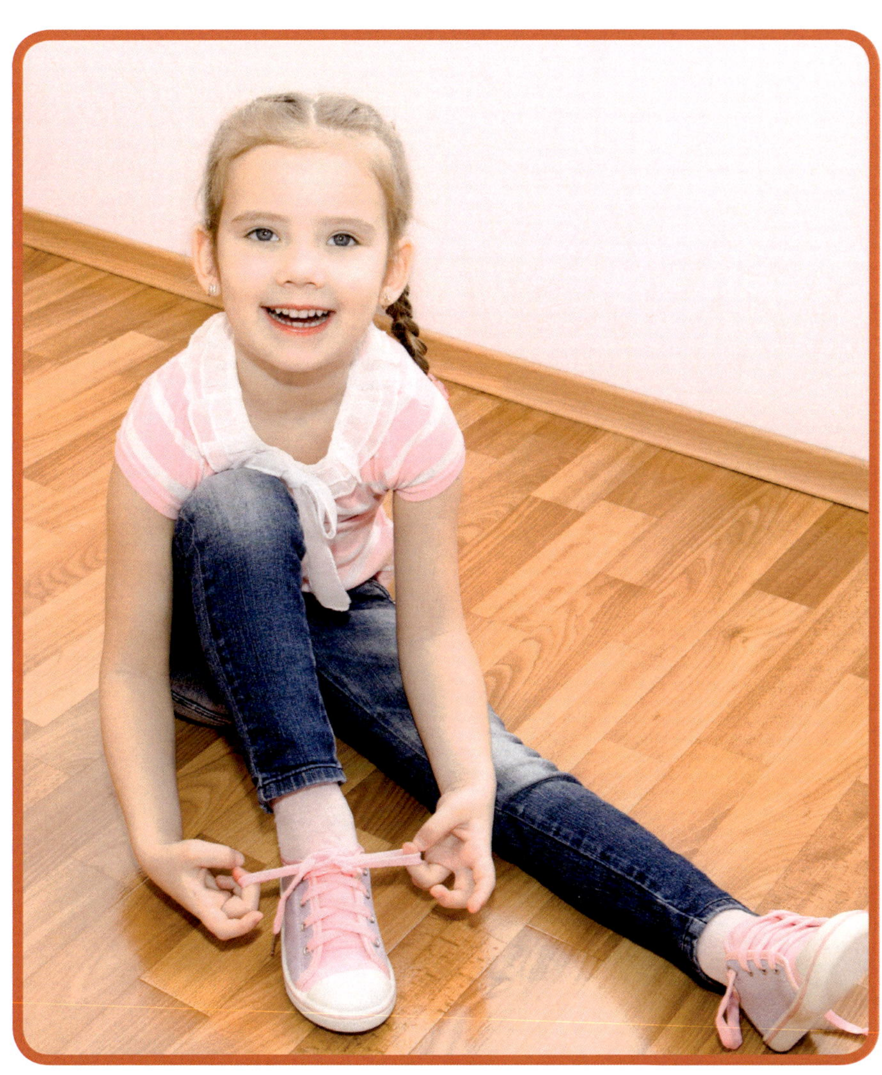

I tie.

Words to Know

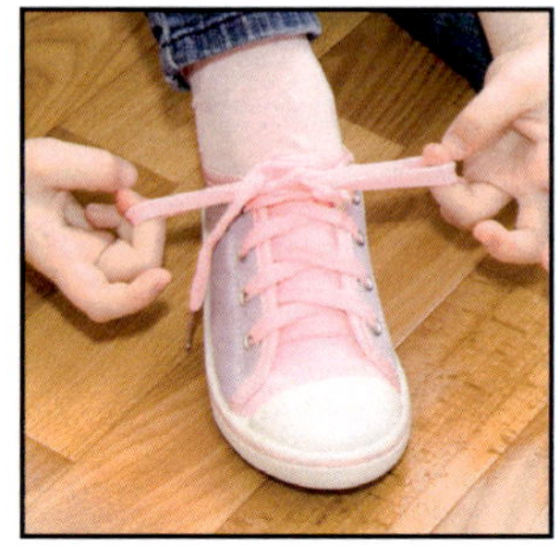

tie

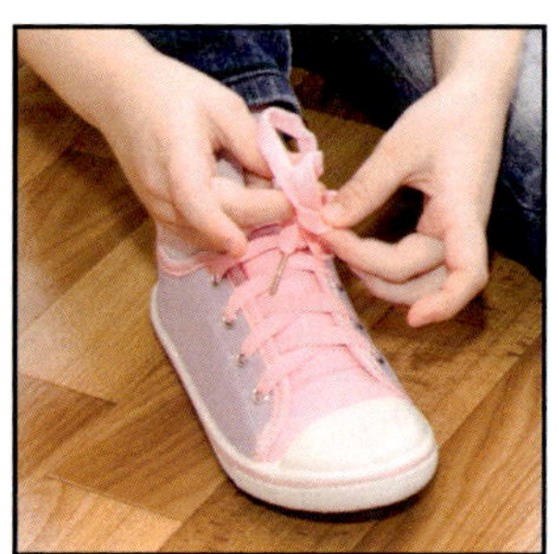

tuck